GUITAR GENIUS

HOW LES PAUL ENGINEERED THE SOLID-BODY ELECTRIC GUITAR AND ROCKED THE WORLD

BY
KIM TOMSIC

ILLUSTRATED BY
BRETT HELQUIST

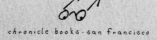

chronicle books · san francisco

In a three-story schoolhouse near the Fox River in Waukesha, Wisconsin, children scrambled into the music room.

Tambourines shimmied, drums boomed, and bells clanged. Little Lester loved it all—the punchy pluck of banjo chords, the bright twinkle of piano keys, and the rise and fall of notes.

Lester couldn't read the music sheets. Those tracks of squiggly lines and black dots didn't make sense. But it didn't matter. The fun part was all the sounds he could make.

At his after-school piano lesson,
his teacher sighed and pinned a note to
his shirt.

He skipped all the way home.

"What does it say?" he asked, grinning from freckle to freckle.

"Well," Lester's mother said gently. "It says you'll never be musical."

Lester's shoulders sank. His eyes stung.

"Don't listen to her." His mother tore the paper into tiny pieces. "You are going to be great."

"Really?"

"You can do anything you put your mind to."

Lester thought about that.

He did a lot of thinking. One day while he was stuffing newspapers for his paper route, his buddy, Harry, showed up wrapping wire around an empty oatmeal can.

"What are you doing, Harry?"

"I'm building a crystal radio set."

Well, that was interesting. So Lester gathered bits and parts and built his own crystal kit. Then he wired it right to the bedsprings in his mattress for an antenna . . .

Out from his home-built radio floated the warm drawl of guitar strings. *Wowza!*

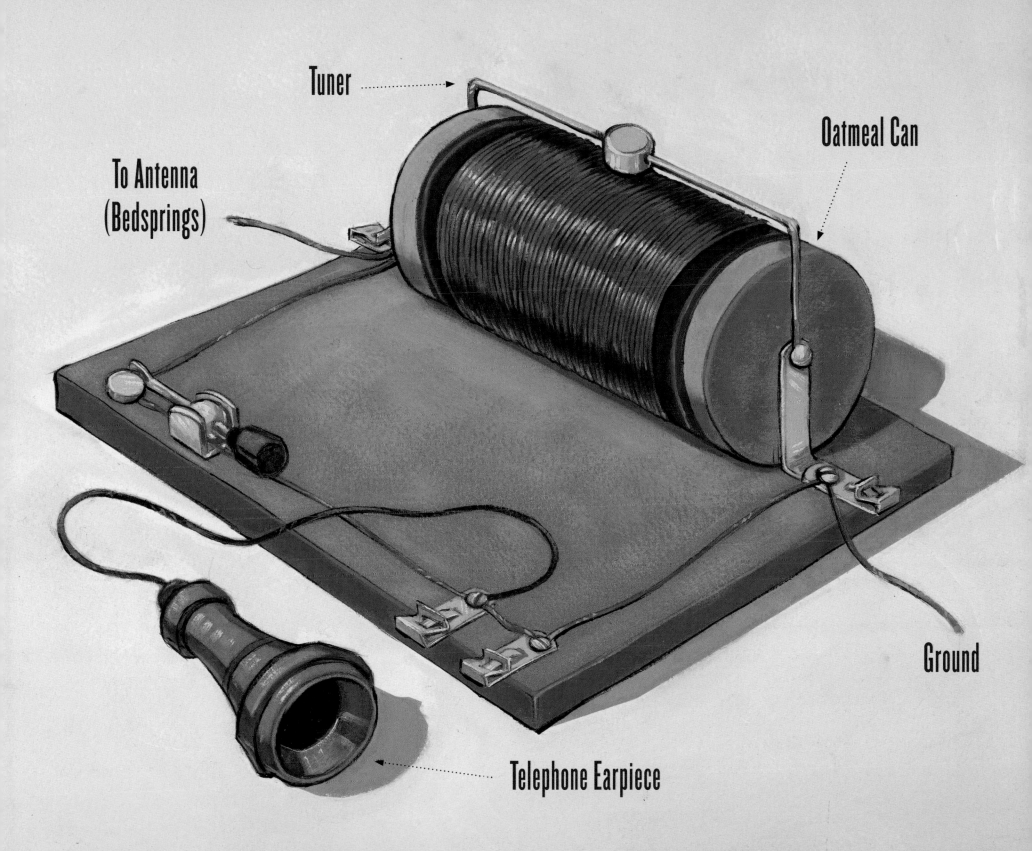

Tuner

Oatmeal Can

To Antenna
(Bedsprings)

Ground

Telephone Earpiece

Lester saved his paper route earnings until he had enough to order his very own guitar.

As Lester opened the box, his finger hit one of the guitar strings.

"You already sound great, Lester!" his mother said.

He didn't. Lester fumbled through the chords. His fingers floundered over the fret board. He even blundered through the B notes. His hands weren't big enough to reach all six strings, so he removed one. And then he practiced and practiced until . . .

He could play the guitar, the banjo, and even the harmonica. He sounded so slick that the manager of WTMJ invited him to play on the radio!

"Mister," his mother said, "you don't know how good that sounds. I wish you could hear it like we do when you play on the radio."

Lester wished that, too, but he didn't own a recording device. It was the 1920s. Nobody he knew owned that sort of gadget. But that was okay. If he didn't have a recording device, he'd build one.

He scrutinized the family's newfangled gizmos, tinkering in his mother's living room and his father's garage. And then he took everything apart—things like the phonograph, the player piano, the telephone, and the radio.

"Ma," his big brother hollered. "The kid's at it again!"

"Leave him alone, Ralph," his mother said. "He's just trying to learn."

Nail

With a Cadillac flywheel, a dentist's belt, a nail, and other pieces and parts, he built a recording lathe so he could record his music.

He made recordings of his guitar strumming and harmonica humming, and then he played them back to figure out how to make it sound better. Soon, he could whip out all sorts of knee-slapping, hillbilly melodies. Everybody said he was super.

But Lester wanted to be even better. He wanted to play *both* sides of his harmonica while he plucked his guitar.

"You only have two arms, you goofus," Ralph said. "You can't flip a harmonica and play a guitar at the same time. Everyone knows that's impossible."

But Lester thought it *was* possible.

So when Ralph left for work at the neighborhood dry cleaning store, Lester picked up a coat hanger left lying around the house.

He fitted the hanger over his shoulders, and shaped the other ends to fit the harmonica so he could flip the instrument with his chin and play twice as many sounds.

Hot dog! It worked. He could hum and strum at the same time.

At thirteen years old, Lester called himself Red Hot Red. He landed local gigs by playing his guitar-harmonica act and telling funny stories. He performed for tips at nearby movie theaters, clubs, and drive-ins.

Folks who sat up front loved the act, but people in the back complained. "We can't hear you, Red! Nobody in the back can hear you play!"

Lester wanted his music heard up front, in back, and in the way, WAY back. His tips depended on it!

He thought and thought until a solution struck him. He could make it louder! All he had to do was borrow a few things from home—a cinderblock, a broomstick, a telephone, and a radio.

He stuffed the broom handle into the cinderblock, and mounted the telephone's mouthpiece to the top of the broom handle. *There!* A microphone stand! Then he wired it to the radio to create the speaker for his sound.

Lester sang and played his harmonica into the homemade mic. Sure enough, the tune boomed from the speaker.

Hooray! Folks in the front could hear. Folks in the back could hear. But a heckler in the way, WAY back sent a note to Lester. It read: *Red, your voice is fine, your harmonica's fine, and your jokes are funny, but the guitar is not loud enough.*

Lester rummaged through the garage until a brilliant idea zipped to mind—to take the tone-arm off his father's phonograph player and jam the arm with the needle into the top of the guitar.

He taped everything in place and wired it to his dad's radio.

"Geez," Ralph said, staring at the ruined phonograph. "What did you do that for?"

"If it plays a phonograph record, it must play a guitar, right? They both vibrate." He snatched up the contraption and headed back to Beekman's Bar-B-Q to test it in front of a crowd.

It worked! Harmonica sounds floated from one radio speaker—*bazzooie-buzzlebahhh*. Guitar strumming amplified from the other radio speaker—*strum-twang, strum twaaaaang*. EVERYONE could hear. It was a smashing success! Almost. The problem was it wasn't just the strings vibrating—the hollow space in the middle of the guitar vibrated, too, making the speaker echo and *screeeeeeeeeech*.

Lester knew he could play cleaner tones if he could just stop the guitar from vibrating. *How, though?* It bamboozled him.

He tried stuffing the hollow center with rags, socks, and a tablecloth. Nope. Next, he filled it with plaster of Paris—that was a bust (and a ruined guitar). Lester had one more idea. He borrowed a wagon and convinced four friends to trek down a steep riverbank to the railroad tracks to help him. There he found a two-and-a-half-foot piece of discarded steel rail.

Back at home, he attached a guitar string to the rail and placed a telephone microphone under the string to pick up the sound vibrations.

"Now what are you doing?" Ralph asked.

"There's only one way to do this," Lester said. "Steel is dense and free of the vibrations I don't want."

He gave his steel guitar a strum. *Wah-wah-wah, Bow-chicka-bow-woooow!*

"Yowzer!" Ralph said.

But his mom, who usually thought Lester was the cat's meow, shook her head and frowned. "That'll be the day when you see a cowboy sitting on a horse playing a railroad track."

All the cowboys in the movies and traveling shows played guitars. *Shucks*, guitars and cowboys went together like peanut butter and jelly! If a cowboy wouldn't like this idea, then nobody would.

"Rats!" But Lester pushed on.

He tweaked and tinkered until he found a way to amplify his acoustic guitar without echo and feedback. *TWAAAAANG!* It sounded okay. *Good*, even. But it wasn't the rich sound he'd heard the steel rail play.

He continued practicing, and when he turned seventeen, his mom let him take his act on the road.

RHUBARB RED

At nineteen years old, he shortened his name from Lester Polsfuss to Les Paul. A few years after that, he formed a band called the Les Paul Trio. He played hillbilly music in the daytime (as Rhubarb Red) and later learned blues and jazz at night (as the Wizard of Waukesha). He swapped licks on his guitar in Chicago and then in New York beside some of the greatest musicians of the time. The new style of music got Les's mind ticking again. He loved the variety of sounds—the *vibrato* of clarinets, the *badum-tishhhh* of drums, the *blurp* of horns. But the *TWAAAAANG* of his guitar still wasn't loud enough.

Louis Armstrong

Charlie Christian

Art Tatum

The Les Paul Trio

Coleman Hawkins

Bing Crosby

Nat King Cole

By the time Les turned twenty-four, he'd become a hotsy-totsy musician. Even President Franklin D. Roosevelt loved his tunes when Les and his razz-matazz-jazz trio performed at the White House.

Still, Les dreamed of the sound of that iron rail—how could he make an electric guitar that held a note like that? The question prickled and pestered in his mind, until 1941, when he was twenty-six years old.

He didn't have equipment or a workshop. Nothing.

4x4

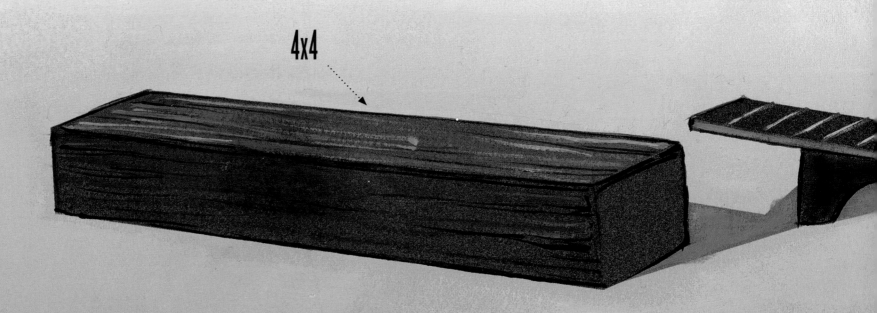

But he was Red Hot Red, Rhubarb Red, the Wizard of Waukesha. He could do anything he set his mind to.

The night watchman at the Epiphone guitar factory let him in on Sundays. There, he took a 4x4 piece of solid pine, hooked on an Epiphone neck, his own homemade pickups, and guitar strings. His solid-body electric guitar looked like a log with strings on it, so he called it "The Log."

And when he gave it a strum—*Wah-wah-wah, Bow-chicka-bow-wooow!*

"Hot dog!" Les said. It was the best thing he'd ever heard!

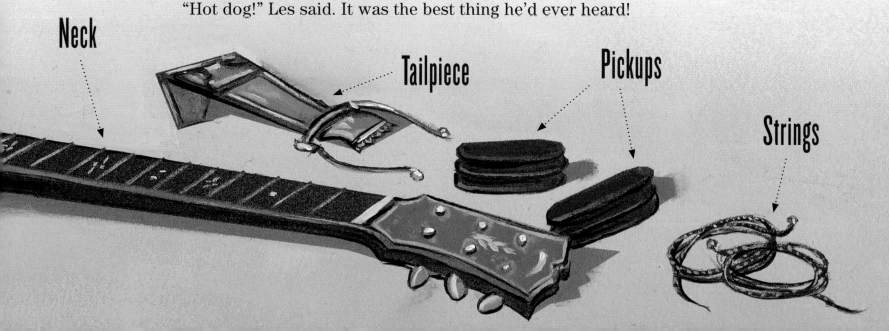

He took it to a swanky nightclub to show off his new sound. But when he played the Log in front of a crowd, they didn't applaud. They didn't boo. Folks just looked at one another. "What is that thing?"

Huh? How could the audience not hear what he heard?

But Les's shoulders didn't sink. His eyes didn't get stingy. He did not give up.

Maybe the audience hears with its eyes?

Les returned to the Epiphone factory and told the watchman, "Everyone's confused. They don't know it's a guitar."

"There!" Les said. "Now it looks more like a guitar."

But it *wasn't* a regular guitar—it was a solid-body electric guitar. *Wah-wah-wah, Bow-chicka-bow-wooow!* It purred! It hummed! It twanged in all the right ways! Finally, the sound he'd dreamed of had come alive. The crowd went wild.

No matter what anyone told Les, he never stopped working on all kinds of sound. His hard work earned him a place in the Rock & Roll Hall of Fame, the Grammy Hall of Fame, and many other halls of fame. He also received the Trustees Award from the National Academy of Recording Arts & Sciences.

At eighty-nine, Les Paul was inducted into the National Inventors Hall of Fame. When he walked on stage to receive his award, noise erupted and boomed from the crowd. *Clapppity-clapclap, Rooooooar, Huzzahhhhhh, Hoorahhhhhh, Hoorayyyyyyy!*

Hot dog, Les thought.

FROM THE AUTHOR

It's only fair to mention that in the early 1930s a musician named George Beauchamp and an electrical engineer named Adolph Rickenbacker teamed up to create the first commercially viable amplifiable electric guitar (the Frying Pan). To many, Les is considered the father of the solid-body electric guitar—U.S. Patent No. 3,018,680, a design many musicians consider unmatched in sound and prowess. The National Inventors Hall of Fame lists Les Paul as the man who "introduced the world to the solid-body electric guitar, a pioneering instrument that transformed popular music."

Perseverance is one of the most admirable attributes about Lester William Polsfuss. Les never learned how to read sheet music. He spent his life playing "by ear," which meant he had to listen carefully and then figure out how to play the sounds. It's hard to believe his piano teacher really sent that discouraging note home, but according to Les, the entire note said, *Your boy, Lester, will never learn music, so save your money. Please don't send him for any more lessons.* Fortunately, young Les had grit and a mother who absolutely believed in him.

It didn't matter to his mother that Les disassembled home gadgets, punched holes in the player piano roll, or even that he cut out a bit of the staircase. His mother thought everything he did was brilliant. As the Les Paul Foundation's website notes, "Each night when young Lester headed up the stairs to bed, he would play his 'wooden xylophone,' which is how he described the vertical planks along the stairs. Lester explained, '[There] was a problem. The xylophone was out of tune, so I had to tune it. I cut the bottom of the plank that was out of tune.' Les shared that his mother thought he was a genius for being able to 'tune' the staircase."

In the 1940s, Leo Fender and Les Paul were dear friends. Fender and Paul Bigsby regularly hung out with Les in his backyard. Les showed them the Log. The three inventors knew the solid-body electric guitar was the future and they talked about it all the time. Fender invited Les to partner in producing an electric guitar. Les declined—he wanted to hold out for a deal with Gibson. In 1948, Fender went on to create the Telecaster, first called the Broadcaster. After Fender's success with the Telecaster, Gibson finally teamed up with Les and in 1952 produced the Gibson *Les Paul* solid-body electric guitar. As for Paul Bigsby—he also built custom electric guitars in the 40s, but he gained fame for the Bigsby vibrato tailpieces.

Les's desire for the perfect sound didn't stop at the guitar. The Rock & Roll Hall of Fame website says, "He also refined the technology of sound recording, developing revolutionary engineering techniques such as close-miking, echo delay, overdubbing, and multitracking." The Les Paul Foundation notes, "Les Paul's contributions to the music industry are legion—tape delay, phasing effects, multi-track recording, and overdubbing, or Sound on Sound—all techniques that . . . have helped to evolve music and recording technology over the past half-century. Of these, his Sound on Sound was the most revolutionary—never before had recording allowed, or been used for, making multiple recorded tracks that could be played in tandem, creating a whole new sonic world for musicians and engineers to explore."

Musicians of various backgrounds sing the praises of Les Paul. In 1988, when B.B. King and Les Paul performed together at Brooklyn Academy, B.B. King said, "Finally, we get together and I get a chance to meet what I think is a legend in his own time." B.B. King later remembered that meeting, calling Les one of his heroes. In an interview for "Chasing Sound," Bonnie Raitt talks about how much she appreciates Les Paul's invention of multitracking and says, "I mean that to me—the greatest thing invented—multitracking. We couldn't have records without it. I couldn't write music without it." Guitarist Rick Derringer said, "He was really an innovator in modern recording techniques. It's almost like he was the person who invented the sound of today's pop records."

Les never stopped pursuing the contraptions of his imagination. He didn't stop when he almost electrocuted himself in 1941 and had to be bandaged from head to toe—he just worked harder. When he shattered his right arm in a car accident in 1948, doctors wanted to amputate, but with the can-do attitude he had all his life, he convinced them to set his arm at a right angle, so he could keep whipping out licks on his guitar. In the 1950s, he created the "Les Paulverizer"—a remote control attached to his guitar to let him play pre-recorded layers of songs, so that during live performances he could produce his multitrack sound. In simple terms, he could play several parts of music at the same time, and in fact, his song "Lover" features Les playing eight different guitar parts! He used his revolutionary Sound on Sound recording methods to produce songs for Capitol Records right in his living room, in hotel rooms, and in bathrooms. Furthermore, Les designed the eight-track tape recorder (marketed by Ampex). Not only was he a great inventor, Les Paul was an incredible guitarist. Lester, the kid who would "never learn music," went on to win seven Grammy Awards.

Les Paul's discoveries in sound changed the landscape of music. Casual music listeners may not know this, but most accomplished musicians will tell you: Music as we hear it would not exist without Les Paul's perseverance and groundbreaking innovations and inventions.

WORKS CITED

Arntz, James. *Les Paul: Chasing Sound*. Icon Television Music, 2007.

Cooke, Alistair, and Robert Saudek. "Omnibus." *Omnibus*, CBS, 1953.

Flatow, Ira. "Les Paul: Inventor and Innovator." *Science Friday*, NPR, Sept. 27, 2013.

Gugliotta, Guy. "'The Log' Puts Paul in Ranks of Top Inventors." *The Washington Post*, May 16, 2005, www.washingtonpost.com/wp-dyn/content/article/2005/05/15/AR2005051500649.html.

"Home - Les Paul Foundation." *LesPaul.com*, Les Paul Foundation, www.lespaulfoundation.org/.

"The Inventions—Les Paul." *LesPaul.com*, Les Paul Foundation, www.les-paul.com/timeline/les-the-inventor/.

Lawrence, Robb. *The Early Years of the Les Paul Legacy: 1915–1963*. Winona: Hal Leonard, 2008.

"Les Paul." National Inventors Hall of Fame, 2005, m.invent.org/honor/inductees/inductee-detail/?IID=225.

"Les Paul." *PBS*, Public Broadcasting Service, Sept. 2, 2008, www.pbs.org/wnet/americanmasters/les-paul-career-timeline/101/.

"Les Paul." Rock & Roll Hall of Fame, Rock & Roll Hall of Fame Archives, www.rockhall.com/inductees/les-paul.

Orentreich, Catherine and Susan Brockman, directors. *The Wizard of Waukesha : the Film about Les Paul*. Stray Cat Productions/USA Nightflight, 1980.

Paul, Les, and Michael Cochran. *Les Paul: In His Own Words*. Timonium: Gemstone Publishing, 2009.

Sue Baker (Program Director, Les Paul Foundation), interviews conducted by the author via phone and email, Dec. 2015–Sept. 2017.

Uebelherr , Jan, and Jackie Loohauis-Bennett. "Exit, Wizard of Waukesha." *Journal Sentinel* (USA Today Network), Aug. 13, 2009, archive.jsonline.com/news/waukesha/53141582.html/.

Walker, Don. "Guitar Legend Les Paul Dies at 94." *PopMatters*, *Milwaukee Journal Sentinel*, Aug. 13, 2009, www.popmatters.com/article/109835-guitar-legend-les-paul-dies-at-94/.

For Cayman Tomsic, my guitar hero—K. T.
For Woody, my guitar teacher—B. H.

Library of Congress Cataloging-in-Publication Data:

Names: Tomsic, Kim, author. | Helquist, Brett, illustrator.
Title: Guitar genius : how Les Paul engineered the solid-body
electric guitar and rocked the world /
  by Kim Tomsic ; illustrated by Brett Helquist.
Description: San Francisco, California : Chronicle Books, [2019] |
Includes bibliographical references.
Identifiers: LCCN 2017045870 | ISBN 9781452159195 (alk. paper)
Subjects: LCSH: Paul, Les—Juvenile literature. | Guitarists—
United States—Biography—Juvenile literature. | Inventors—
United States—Biography—Juvenile literature.
Classification: LCC ML3930.P29 T66 2019 | DDC 787.87092 [B] —
dc23 LC record available at https://lccn.loc.gov/2017045870

Manufactured in China.

Design by Ryan Hayes.
Typeset in ITC Century & Knockout.
The illustrations in this book were rendered in oil paint
on watercolor paper.

10 9 8 7 6 5 4 3 2 1

Chronicle Books LLC
680 Second Street
San Francisco, California 94107

Chronicle Books—we see things differently. Become
part of our community at www.chroniclekids.com.

ACKNOWLEDGMENTS

It is with deep gratitude that I start by thanking Sue Baker and the Les Paul Foundation. Thank you, Sue, for the generosity of your time and for your excitement for this book. Because of your friendship with Les, you were able to share treasured details that helped this book come alive. I have had so much fun talking and emailing with you. As you say, Les Paul truly is the never-ending story!

Thank you to my son Cayman Tomsic for introducing me to the name Les Paul and for setting me on the journey to write this book. Thank you for sharing the magic of your skills on drums, mandolin, ukulele, acoustic guitar, and electric guitar. Your music has filled our house with joy.

Thank you to Steve Mesple, owner of Wildwood Guitars, and to John Brandow for answering my questions and providing a fun space to see any guitar our hearts desired. And special thanks to Ron Aguiar for chatting about Les Paul and for letting Cayman play your Black Beauty.

Thank you to my critiquing group members: Brian Papa, Sally Spear, Denise Vega, Lauren Sabel, Elaine Pease, Penny Berman, and Will James Limón. Man, I'm lucky to know you!

Thank you to my dynamic agent Jennifer Rofé and my brilliant editor Melissa Manlove. You guys rock!

Thank you to Lin Oliver and Steve Mooser for starting the SCBWI. I would not understand the craft or business of children's literature without this organization.

A special thank you to early readers, overall supporters, and/or neighbors (who loved us through 10 years of loud music): Celia Sinoway, Kevin Orin, Karen and Jim Churnside, Joseph Provost, Jerilyn Patterson, and Aspen Nolan.

Thank you Steve Tomsic and Noelle Tomsic for your never-ending enthusiasm and support.

For more about the Les Paul Foundation, visit www.lespaulfoundation.org.